STRETCHY SHAPES!
Straight, Curved, and Twisty

By BLAKE HOENA
Illustrated by GLENN THOMAS
Music by ERIK KOSKINEN

CANTATA
LEARNING

WWW.CANTATALEARNING.COM

CANTATA
LEARNING

Published by Cantata Learning
1710 Roe Crest Drive
North Mankato, MN 56003
www.cantatalearning.com

Library of Congress Cataloging-in-Publication Data
Names: Hoena, B. A., author. | Thomas, Glenn, illustrator. | Koskinen, Erik
composer.
Title: Stretchy shapes : straight, curved, and twisty / by Blake Hoena ;
illustrated by Glenn Thomas ; music by Erik Koskinen.
Description: North Mankato, MN : Cantata Learning, 2019. | Series: Creative
movement | Audience: K to Grade 3.
Identifiers: LCCN 2017056293 (print) | LCCN 2018001775 (ebook) | ISBN
9781684102709 (eBook) | ISBN 9781684102457 (hardcover : alk. paper)
Subjects: LCSH: Physical fitness for children--Juvenile literature. |
Stretching exercises--Juvenile literature.
Classification: LCC GV443 (ebook) | LCC GV443 .H565 2019 (print) | DDC
613.7/042--dc23
LC record available at https://lccn.loc.gov/2017056293'

Book design and art direction, Tim Palin Creative
Editorial direction, Kellie M. Hultgren
Music direction, Elizabeth Draper
Music arranged and produced by Erik Koskinen

Printed in the United States of America.
0390

ACCESS THE MUSIC!
SCAN CODE WITH MOBILE APP
CANTATALEARNING.COM

TIPS TO SUPPORT LITERACY AT HOME

WHY READING AND SINGING WITH YOUR CHILD IS SO IMPORTANT

Daily reading with your child leads to increased academic achievement. Music and songs, specifically rhyming songs, are a fun and easy way to build early literacy and language development. Music skills correlate significantly with both phonological awareness and reading development. Singing helps build vocabulary and speech development. And reading and appreciating music together is a wonderful way to strengthen your relationship.

READ AND SING EVERY DAY!

TIPS FOR USING CANTATA LEARNING BOOKS AND SONGS DURING YOUR DAILY STORY TIME

1. As you sing and read, point out the different words on the page that rhyme. Suggest other words that rhyme.

2. Memorize simple rhymes such as Itsy Bitsy Spider and sing them together. This encourages comprehension skills and early literacy skills.

3. Use the questions in the back of each book to guide your singing and storytelling.

4. Read the included sheet music with your child while you listen to the song. How do the music notes correlate to the words of the song?

5. Sing along on the go and at home. Access music by scanning the QR code on each Cantata book. You can also stream or download the music for free to your computer, smartphone, or mobile device.

Devoting time to daily reading shows that you are available for your child. Together, you are building language, literacy, and listening skills.

Have fun reading and singing!

What shapes can your body make? When you move your body slowly, it helps keep your muscles **flexible** and strong. Stretching also gets you ready to be **active** and to **exercise**.

Be careful when stretching. You want to do stretches correctly and slowly to keep from getting hurt.

Now turn the page and stretch along to the song!

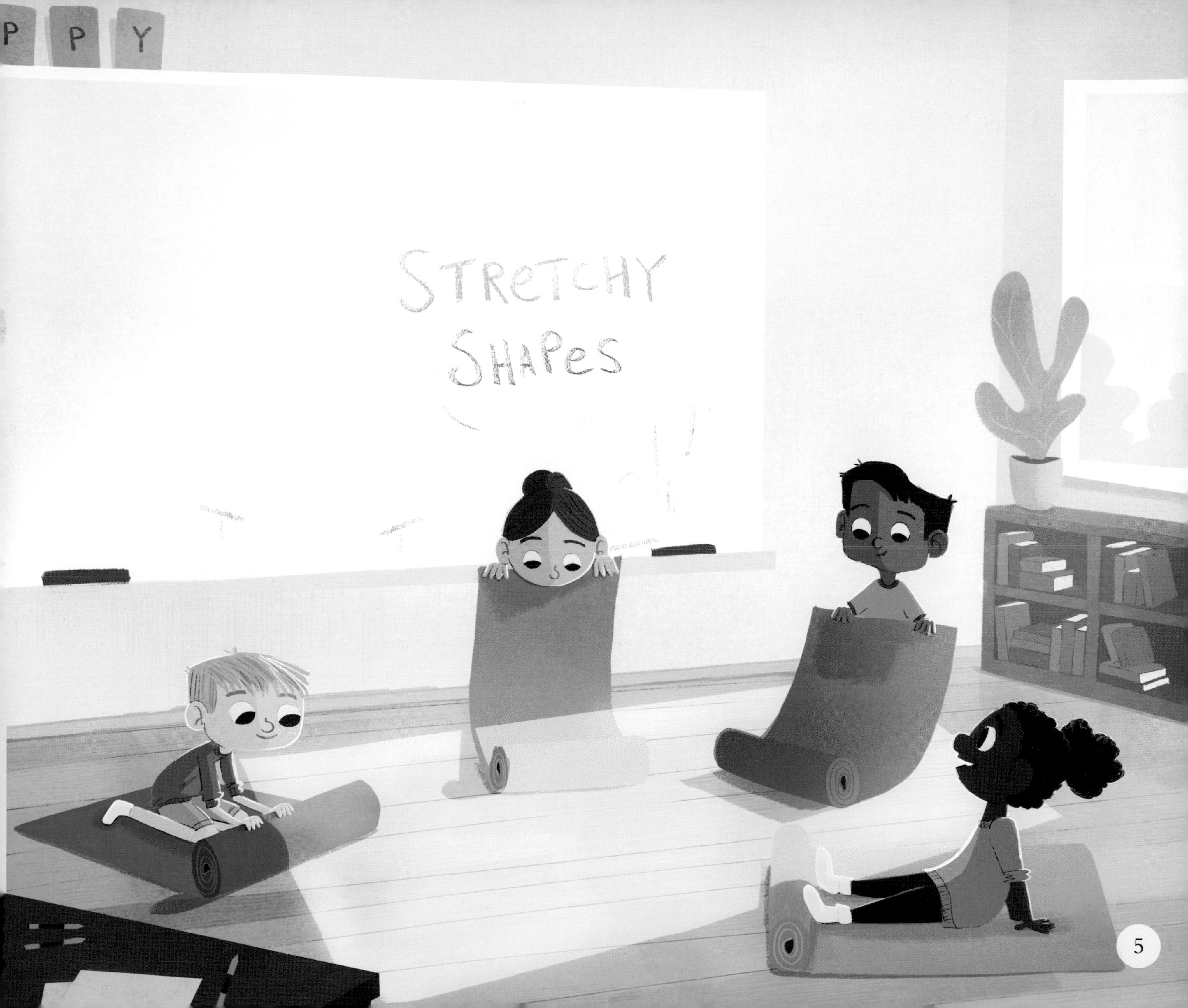
P P Y
STRETCHY
SHAPES

Lie down, down on your back.
Reach your arms up over your head.

Stretch out. Form a straight line,
like you're stretching out in bed.

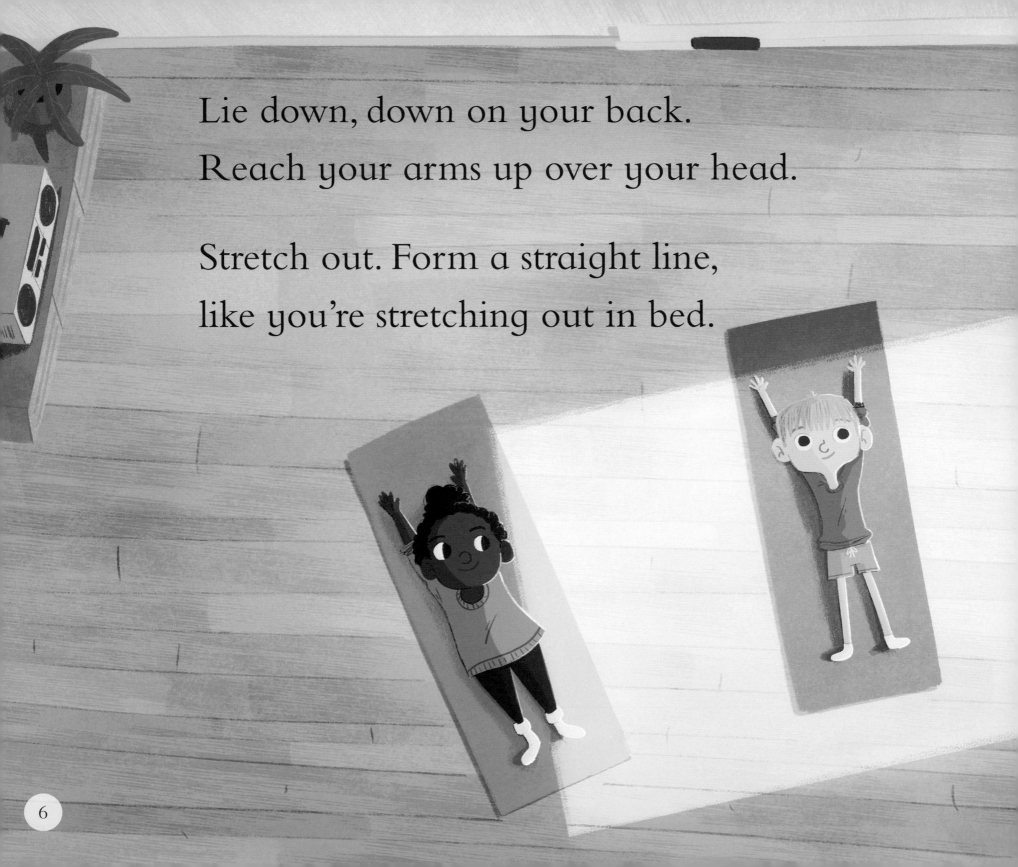

Breathe in as you stretch. Breathe out to **relax**.
Breathe in as you stretch. Breathe out to relax.

Curl up, up in a ball.
Pull your knees tight to your chest.

Now rock, rock back and forth.
Stretching slowly is the best.

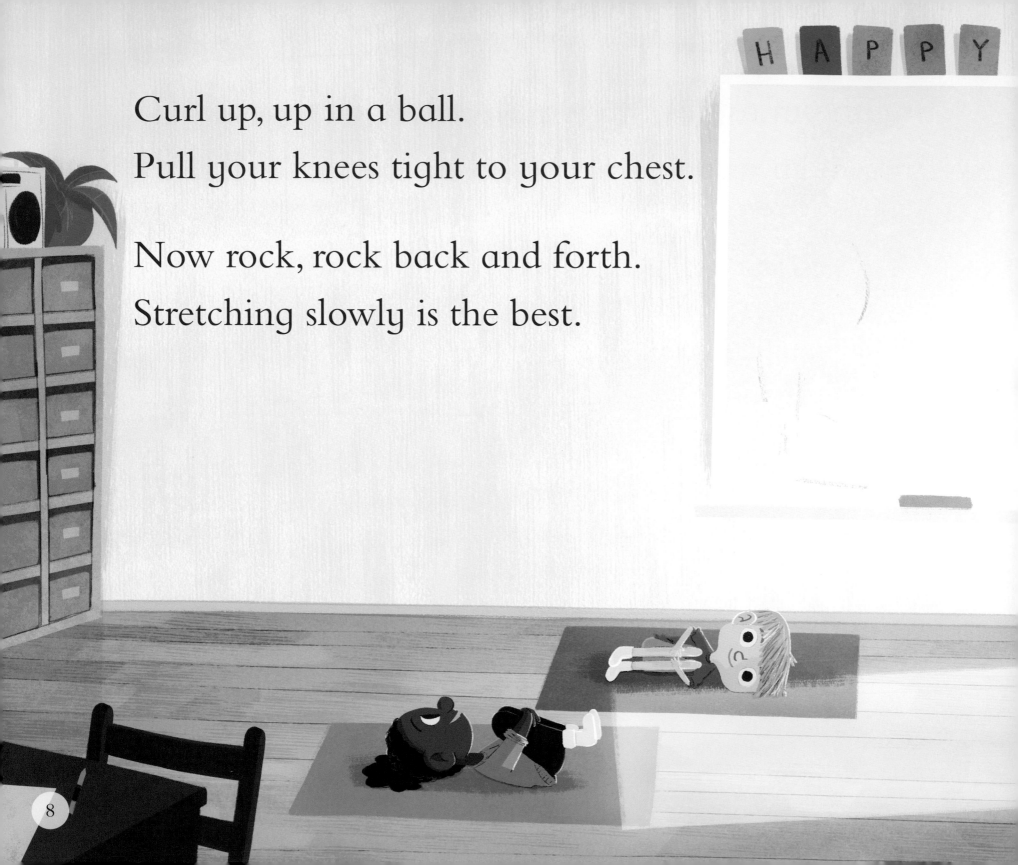

HAPPY

Breathe in as you stretch. Breathe out to relax.

Breathe in as you stretch. Breathe out to relax.

Now roll to your hands and knees.
Curve your back up to the sky.

Then **arc**, arc your belly down
to the ground. Give it a try!

Breathe in as you stretch. Breathe out to relax.
Breathe in as you stretch. Breathe out to relax.

Lift up. Lift your hips up.
Your body forms a triangle.

Be still, just for a bit.
Now start to stretch and wiggle.

HAPPY

Breathe in as you stretch. Breathe out to relax.
Breathe in as you stretch. Breathe out to relax.

Stand up, up on your feet.
Put your hands upon your waist.

Now circle your hips around,
standing there in one place.

Breathe in as you stretch. Breathe out to relax.
Breathe in as you stretch. Breathe out to relax.

Now spread, spread your feet apart.
Spread your arms to form a star.

Reach up, up with one hand,
then the other hand. It's not hard!

Breathe in as you stretch. Breathe out to relax.

Breathe in as you stretch. Breathe out to relax.

Sit down, down on the ground
with your legs in front of you.

Now bend, bend at your waist.
Stretch your fingers toward your shoes.

Breathe in as you stretch. Breathe out to relax.
Breathe in as you stretch. Breathe out to relax.

Lie down, down on your back.

Put your hands upon your chest.

Breathe in. Slowly breathe out.

Stay still, it's time to rest.

Breathe in as you stretch. Breathe out to relax.

Breathe in as you stretch. Breathe out to relax.

21

SONG LYRICS
Stretchy Shapes! Straight, Curved, and Twisty

Lie down, down on your back.
Reach your arms up over your head.

Stretch out. Form a straight line,
like you're stretching out in bed.

Breathe in as you stretch.
    Breathe out to relax.
Breathe in as you stretch.
    Breathe out to relax.

Curl up, up in a ball.
Pull your knees tight to your chest.

Now rock, rock back and forth.
Stretching slowly is the best.

Breathe in as you stretch.
    Breathe out to relax.
Breathe in as you stretch.
    Breathe out to relax.

Now roll to your hands and knees.
Curve your back up to the sky.

Then arc, arc your belly down
to the ground. Give it a try!

Breathe in as you stretch.
    Breathe out to relax.

Breathe in as you stretch.
    Breathe out to relax.

Lift up. Lift your hips up.
Your body forms a triangle.

Be still, just for a bit.
Now start to stretch and wiggle.

Breathe in as you stretch.
    Breathe out to relax.
Breathe in as you stretch.
    Breathe out to relax.

Stand up, up on your feet.
Put your hands upon your waist.

Now circle your hips around,
standing there in one place.

Breathe in as you stretch.
    Breathe out to relax.
Breathe in as you stretch.
    Breathe out to relax.

Now spread, spread your feet apart.
Spread your arms to form a star.

Reach up, up with one hand,
then the other hand. It's not hard!

Breathe in as you stretch.
    Breathe out to relax.
Breathe in as you stretch.
    Breathe out to relax.

Sit down, down on the ground
with your legs in front of you.

Now bend, bend at your waist.
Stretch your fingers toward your shoes.

Breathe in as you stretch.
    Breathe out to relax.
Breathe in as you stretch.
    Breathe out to relax.

Lie down, down on your back.
Put your hands upon your chest.

Breathe in. Slowly breathe out.
Stay still, it's time to rest.

Breathe in as you stretch.
    Breathe out to relax.
Breathe in as you stretch.
    Breathe out to relax.

Stretchy Shapes! Straight, Curved, and Twisty

Americana
Erik Koskinen

Verse

1. Lie down, down on your back. Reach your arms up o-ver your head. Stretch out. Form a straight line, like you're stretch-ing out in bed.

Chorus

Breathe in as you stretch. Breathe out to re - lax. Breathe in as you stretch. Breathe out to re - lax. lax.

Verse 2
Curl up, up in a ball.
Pull your knees tight to your chest.
Now rock, rock back and forth.
Stretching slowly is the best.

Chorus

Verse 3
Now roll to your hands and knees.
Curve your back up to the sky.
Then arc, arc your belly down
to the ground. Give it a try!

Chorus

Verse 4
Lift up. Lift your hips up.
Your body forms a triangle.
Be still, just for a bit.
Now start to stretch and wiggle.

Chorus

Verse 5
Stand up, up on your feet.
Put your hands upon your waist.
Now circle your hips around,
standing there in one place.

Chorus

Verse 6
Now spread, spread your feet apart.
Spread your arms to form a star.
Reach up, up with one hand,
then the other hand. It's not hard!

Chorus

Verse 7
Sit down, down on the ground
with your legs in front of you.
Now bend, bend at your waist.
Stretch your fingers toward your shoes.

Chorus

Verse 8
Lie down, down on your back.
Put your hands upon your chest.
Breathe in. Slowly breathe out.
Stay still, it's time to rest.

Chorus

GLOSSARY

active—moving

arc—curve into a half circle

exercise—action for physical fitness

flexible—able to bend easily

relax—rest

CRITICAL THINKING QUESTIONS

1. Why do you think the author named this book *Stretchy Shapes! Straight, Curved, and Twisty*?

2. Look back at each illustration. See how the students are moving in each picture. What muscles do you think they are stretching?

3. Think of other shapes that you can create with your body. Make the shape of a tree. Make the shape of a bird. What other shapes can you stretch your body into?

TO LEARN MORE

Cleland, Jo. *Get Moving*. Vero Beach, FL: Rourke, 2013.

Dahl, Michael. *Locomotion! March, Hop, Skip, Gallop, Run*. North Mankato, MN: Cantata Learning, 2019.

Hoena, Blake. *This Is the Way We Move*. North Mankato, MN: Capstone, 2016.

Schuh, Mari. *Get Moving!* North Mankato, MN: Capstone, 2013.